FOOD CHAINS

ALVIN SILVERSTEIN • VIRGINIA SILVERSTEIN • LAURA SILVERSTEIN NUNN

TWENTY-FIRST CENTURY BOOKS

BROOKFIELD, CONNECTICUT

Cover photograph courtesy of Photo Researchers (© Tom and Pat Leeson)

Photographs courtesy of Animals Animals: pp. 4 (© Mickey Gibson), 28
(top © Ray Richardson), 35 (© Henry Ausloos), 42 (© Scott W. Smith), 51 (© J. R. Williams);
The National Audubon Society Collection/Photo Researchers: pp. 7, 10 (© Gregory Ochocki), 13
(© Mark N. Boulton), 19 (© Tim Davis), 20 (© Mitch Reardon), 21 (© Neil S. McDaniel), 24
(© Alan Carey), 28 (2nd from bottom © Betty B. Derig; bottom © Herb Levart); 32 (© Ray Simons),
46 (Lawrence Radiationn Laboratory, Nevada), 49 (© Charles D. Winters);
SuperStock: pp. 9 (© D. C. Lowe), 16 (© David Middleton); Minden Pictures: p. 28
(2nd from top © Michael Quinton); Corbis-Bettmann: p. 39

Library of Congress Cataloging-in-Publication Data

Silverstein, Alvin.
Food Chains / Alvin Silverstein, Virginia Silverstein, Laura Silverstein Nunn.
p.   cm. — (Science concepts)
Includes bibliographical references and index.
Summary: Explains various components of a food chain and discusses the
concepts of food webs, umbrella species, biogeochemical cycles, and more.
ISBN 0-7613-3002-X (lib. bdg.)
1. Food chains (Ecology)—Juvenile literature. [1. Food chains (Ecology) 2. Ecology.]
I. Silverstein. Virginia B. II. Nunn, Laura Silverstein. III. Title.
IV. Series: Silverstein, Alvin. Science concepts.
QH541.S534   1998
577' .16—dc21   97-52147
                                                                        CIP
                                                                        AC

Published by Twenty-First Century Books
A Division of The Millbrook Press, Inc.
2 Old New Milford Road
Brookfield, Connecticut 06804

CONTENTS

THE BALANCE OF NATURE

During the early 1900s about four thousand mule deer could be found munching on the leaves, weeds, grass, clover, and mushrooms in the Kaibab National Forest in Arizona, north of the Grand Canyon. The deer population was stable until 1907, when hunters in the area moved to increase the deer population by eliminating their natural predators, such as mountain lions, coyotes, and wolves. The hunters could not have predicted the impact they would have on the environment. By 1924 the deer population increased to an astounding one hundred thousand. These plant-eating animals stripped the land of all its green plant life; they even ate the bark off trees. Their food became scarce, and many starved to death. Deer that wandered into other areas to forage often did not survive. Weakened deer gave birth to stillborn and defective fawns. In 1939 the mule deer population had dramatically declined to about ten thousand.

The Kaibab National Forest is presently a national game preserve, and the wildlife in the area are protected by wildlife officials. The Forest Service has devised a management plan that regulates the size of the mule deer population. The excess deer are killed either by predators or by hunters until there is a balance between the number of deer and the amount of food the land can produce.

✦ A FOOD CONNECTION ✦

All living organisms within an environment are connected through a common link—food. For example, plants need sun, rain, and nutrients from the soil so they can grow. Some animals in the area eat the plants for food. Other animals eat smaller or weaker animals for food. Some animals feed on both plants and animals. Scientists are able to keep track of such relationships by listing the plant and animal species in **food chains**. Basically, a food chain indicates "who eats whom."

Animals and plants that live together in the same area, such as the Kaibab National Forest, belong to a **biological community**. All living organisms in a biological community, including plants and animals, depend on other living and nonliving things in some way. The science that deals with the interdependent relationships among living organisms and their habitat is called **ecology**. The German zoologist Ernst Haeckel coined the term ecology in 1869 from two Greek roots: *oikos,* meaning "household," and *ology,* meaning "study of." He recognized that organisms do not live alone. Instead, they are part of a "household," a community that includes various organisms together with their physical surroundings. A community in which organisms live and interact with each other and their environment is called an **ecosystem**. Ecosystems exist in all the varied places on our planet, from forests, plains, and deserts to lakes, streams, and oceans.

✦ FINDING A NICHE IN SOCIETY ✦

Every organism in a community has a **niche,** a specific role within a community. A niche can be described as a job, or way of living. There are three types of niches: producers, consumers, and decomposers. **Producers** include almost all plants. Their role is to provide food for the other organisms in the community. **Consumers** eat other organisms in the community. Their role is to feed on producers or other consumers or both. For instance, rabbits are consumers because they eat grass and other plants (producers). But foxes are also consumers because they eat rabbits (which are consumers). As one organism feeds on another, which feeds on still another, they are linked into a food chain. Any food chain ends eventually with **decomposers**, which include fungi and bacteria. Their role is to get rid of the dead organisms in the community.

Each link in a food chain must be strong to ensure the survival of all the kinds of organisms involved. When one link is weakened or broken, as happened when most of the mule-deer predators at Kaibab were wiped out, the rest of the food chain is affected either directly or indirectly. A single change in the environment can affect the organisms living in it and thus upset the balance of nature.

Fungi are decomposers, which break down animal and plant matter into compounds that enrich soil. This process also returns carbon dioxide to the air, where green plants use it during photosynthesis.

Energy Flow in Food Chains

What do the sun, a field of grass, a rabbit, and a fox have in common? They are all connected in a food chain. The sun shines on a field of grass and gives it energy to grow. A rabbit comes hopping along, stops to nibble on the grass, and gets energy from the meal. Hiding behind a bush, a fox comes out and tries to catch the rabbit. The rabbit sees the fox and tries to escape. The fox chases the rabbit; the chase ends when the fox catches the rabbit, and it becomes food for the fox, which in turn gets energy from this meal. This food chain illustrates the transfer of energy from one organism to another.

✦ FOOD MAKERS ✦

All living things need energy in order to live. They use energy to breathe, hunt, and reproduce. Almost all the energy that living things on earth use comes originally from the sun. But most creatures cannot use sunlight energy directly. Green plants—whether an oak tree or a dandelion—as well as the algae in a pond or ocean and certain bacteria are the only living organisms that can use sunlight energy to make their own food. They do this through a process called **photosynthesis.**

Photosynthesis, as its name suggests, uses sunlight energy (the *photo-* part of the word) to put simple chemicals together to form more complex ones (a *synthesis*). Plants need water, carbon dioxide, and nitrogen compounds from the

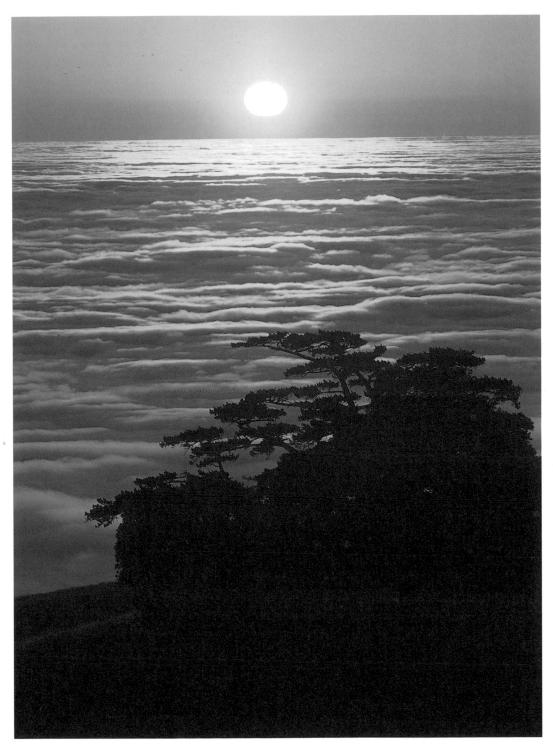

The sun provides the energy for plants to make their own food through photosynthesis.

atmosphere for photosynthesis; using the energy of sunlight, they turn these raw materials into sugars, starches, and other carbohydrates. Green plants get their color from chlorophyll, a green pigment that absorbs sunlight energy that is used to power the chemical reactions of photosynthesis. Part of the sunlight energy is converted to chemical energy, which is stored in the plant's tissues. Photosynthesis takes place both in the water and on land. The need for sunlight is the reason why many water plants live in shallow waters rather than in the deep sea.

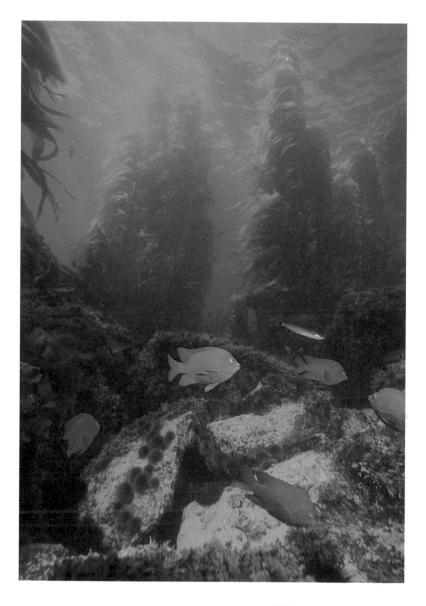

Giant kelp is a form of seaweed. It grows under-water, reaching toward the sunlight that supplies the energy it needs to survive.

Just 500 miles (800 km)southwest of Acapulco, Mexico, and about 1.5 miles (2.5 km) beneath the surface of the Pacific Ocean, a team of researchers in 1991 discovered an interesting biological community where an alternative energy source is used by living things. The sun is necessary for photosynthesis. But sunlight cannot reach the deep sea bottom. However, in this environment, life can grow because there are underwater volcanic fissures, called hydrothermal vents. These vents are like miniature underwater volcanoes. When they "erupt," they kill everything in sight and heat the waters to 400°F (200°C).

But heat is a form of energy. Bacteria that live at the bottom near the vents get heat from the depths of the earth and use its energy and the chemical energy of sulfur compounds in the water to make food. This kind of food production is called **chemosynthesis.** The bacteria continue to grow and flourish. Soon consumers such as crabs and other crustaceans come to feed on the bacteria. Other sea animals, such as tube worms and mussels, feed on the bacteria as well. Within only a year, in this environment without sunlight, the number of species living around the vents can double.

✦ MEMBERS OF A FOOD CHAIN ✦

Producers are the first link in food chains. Plants are producers because they can make their own food through photosynthesis. These photosynthetic organisms are also called **autotrophs,** from the Greek roots for "self-feeders." Autotrophs are the basis of all food chains because they produce food not only for themselves but for all other organisms, either directly or indirectly. For instance, when a rabbit eats grass, it gets the food energy stored in the plants directly. But when a fox eats the rabbit, the fox gets the plant food energy indirectly through the rabbit. And the food energy continues to be passed on up the food chain.

The next links in food chains are consumers, organisms that cannot make their own food and must eat other organisms to live. They are known as **heterotrophs,** from the Greek roots for "other feeders." There are three types of these consumers: herbivores, carnivores, and omnivores. Herbivores, such as grasshoppers, rabbits, deer, and cows, are animals that eat mostly plants. Carnivores, such as foxes and mountain lions, are animals that eat other animals. Carnivores play an important role in food chains because they help to regulate the number of herbivores and thus maintain the balance of nature. Omnivores, such as raccoons and bears, are animals that eat both plants and animals. Most humans are also omnivores. We may have a meal that includes a salad and a steak (producer and consumer).

Decomposers and scavengers form a special group of heterotrophs. Decomposers are organisms, such as fungi and bacteria, that get food by breaking down the remains of dead plants and animals into nutrients. They also break down the waste materials of living organisms. This is an important job because the nutrients enter the soil and help new plants to grow. Scavengers, such as vultures, also feed on the bodies of dead animals. Decomposers and scavengers can be found at every level of the food chain. They get food for themselves and allow materials to be reused by the organisms in the food chains.

✦ KEEPING TRACK OF FOOD ENERGY ✦

A food chain is like a ladder, with animals at each step. The animals at higher levels eat the animals below them. Each step is known as a **trophic level** (from the Greek for "food"). Trophic levels track the transfer of food energy and nourishment among the organisms in an ecosystem. Following a single food chain, we can see how energy moves from one trophic level to the next. For example, a plant that changes energy from the sun into chemical energy during photosynthesis may use part of this energy to form flowers that contain nectar and

A group of vultures can quickly remove the flesh from a dead animal.

pollen. A moth that drinks the flowers' sweet nectar may be snapped up by a frog. Later the frog may be swallowed by a snake, which in turn becomes a meal for a swooping hawk.

NATURE'S POOPER-SCOOPER

Decomposers have a little helper when it comes to cleaning up the environment. In the West African savannahs, a member of the scarab family known as the dung beetle is nature's pooper-scooper. These beetles bury the dung of animals and store it to feed themselves and their families. They work very fast, sometimes burying it within hours. Within a year, the hard-working beetles living on one acre (0.4 hectare) can bury about half a ton of dung.

Dung beetles are significant in the environment, for without their help, the ground would be covered with dung. Minerals and other nutrients in the dung are recycled in the process, providing a natural fertilizer that helps plants to grow.

A compost heap is the perfect environment for decomposers and scavengers. People can recycle plant wastes efficiently by gathering leaves, grass clippings, potato peelings, and other vegetation and putting the material in a compost pile. An effective compost heap consists of layers of organic wastes alternating with thin layers of soil. The mixture is watered to speed up the process. Once the decomposers and scavengers go to work, the bacteria multiply and the organic wastes decay at amazing speeds. The rotting mixture inside a compost heap can reach very high temperatures—up to 130°F (54°C). When the compost is ready, people may use it as a fertilizer to make their gardens more productive or as a mulch around their plants.

The first trophic level begins with the **primary producer** (the flowering plant). The primary producer provides food for the first-level or **primary consumer** (the moth), typically an herbivore. The primary consumer is eaten by the second-level or **secondary consumer** (the frog), which may be a carnivore or omnivore. The secondary consumer is eaten by the third-level or **tertiary consumer** (the snake), which may also be a carnivore or omnivore. Sometimes there may be a fourth-level or **quaternary consumer** (hawk). Some consumers can change levels. For instance, if the hawk eats a mouse that ate seeds, it is a secondary consumer. But the hawk is a tertiary consumer if it eats a mouse that ate insects. When the highest-level consumer in the food chain dies, decomposers and scavengers get rid of it as well as the remains of the other dead organisms at each trophic level.

✦ THREE ✦

THE WEB OF LIFE

What would it be like if animals in the wild ate the same thing day after day? Not only would their life lack variety, but it would also be precarious. What would happen, for example, if lions could eat only zebras? If a natural disaster, such as a raging fire, wiped out the entire zebra population in an area, the lions who lived there would lose their only food source. Soon they, too, would die out. Actually, however, lions will eat many kinds of animals—not only zebras but also antelope, buffalo, warthogs, turtles, and guinea fowl, depending on what prey is available. Their prey, in turn, can feed on a variety of plant life, depending on what is plentiful. Each kind of plant may provide food for a variety of animals. In most ecosystems, there are thus many food chains that are linked together to form a complex **food web**. The diversity of these food webs increases the chances of each species for survival.

The food web, or the "web of life," describes how animals, plants, and other organisms are connected in an ecosystem—how they feed on one another. **Biodiversity**—a variety of species at each trophic level—is essential for the health of a biological community. The more varied an animal's diet, the better chance it has of surviving. A variety of animals eating a particular kind of plant may help to keep it from overgrowing and choking out other plant species. Animals also help plants to reproduce by pollinating their flowers and distributing their seeds.

In the modern world, however, human activities have been decreasing biodiversity. People kill animals and plants they regard as pests, but they can also wipe out species unintentionally. When people clear forests to make farms or build roads and cities, wild creatures lose their food and living space. Pollution from human industries has also damaged natural communities. When species die out, there are far-reaching effects on the other members of their ecosystems. A food web can be compared to a spider web: If a couple of strands are broken, a spider web can still keep its shape. But if too many strands break, the whole web is in danger of collapsing.

✦ THE KEY TO SURVIVAL ✦

Food webs include both strong and weak relationships among species. Some species, called **keystone species,** have a significant effect on their communities. In fact, other members in the community depend on this species for survival. In a building, a keystone is the wedge-shaped piece at the crown of an arch that locks the other pieces in place. Without that "key" piece, everything surrounding it will fall. A mountain lion is a keystone species because it keeps a balance among all living things in its food web. When mountain lions were hunted at the Kaibab National Forest, a disastrous chain reaction was started. Once the mountain lions disappeared from the community, the mule deer multiplied greatly and ate all the available plant material. Soon there was not enough food for everyone, and many animals starved to death.

A mountain lion plays an important part in maintaining the balance among all the species that live in its biological community.

A keystone species can help to maintain diversity within a biological community in two ways. It may control the population of a species that might otherwise multiply wildly, disrupting the balance of nature in the community, the way the mule deer multiplied when the mountain lions were gone; or the keystone species may be a vital resource for a wide range of species. Thus, the keystone species helps to preserve the environment and everything in it, big or small—deer, rabbits, butterflies, plants, and even mosquitoes.

TOO SPECIALIZED

Most animals eat a variety of foods every day. A few animals, however, eat the same food day after day. The koalas of Australia, for instance, can often be found sitting in eucalyptus trees. They eat mostly the leaves and young shoots of these trees. Koalas in the wild do not drink water—they get their liquids from the eucalyptus leaves. Thus, they are completely dependent on the trees. If a disaster destroyed the eucalyptus trees, many koalas would not survive.

The giant panda of central China is already in serious danger for a similar reason. The pandas live in dense bamboo forests, and bamboo shoots and roots make up about 95 percent of their diet. (They also eat flowers, fish, and small rodents.) The panda can get only about 17 percent of the nutrients out of its high-fiber diet; it eats 20 to 40 pounds (9 to 18 kg) of bamboo each day and spends up to 14 hours a day feeding. But commercial development is shrinking the bamboo forests, threatening both the panda's home and its food supply.

In the ocean the shark is a keystone species. The shark has a bad reputation as a murderous beast. But the shark, like the mountain lion, is essential for the survival of all living things in its community. The shark eats a lot of fish and other sea animals. It also helps to keep the ocean waters clean by eating the dead or sick fish. If sharks disappeared from the underwater world, the waters would become dirty and overpopulated with fish. The larger fish would eat all the tiny fish and other water animals that feed on the algae. Then algae would grow so much that the waters would become thick with slime.

WHO'S MORE IMPORTANT?

Who's more important in a biological community—a towering elephant or a tiny fruit bat? The answer: they are equally important. In the rain forest, elephants eat a lot of plants—as much as 500 pounds (225 kg) a day each! This lets sunlight through, helping more plants grow for other animals to eat. Elephants also use their tusks to dig out hard-to-find watering holes, which is necessary during the dry season.

Fruit bats not only eat fruit, but they also plant it. With their tough outer coating, many seeds pass through a bat's digestive system unharmed and fall to the ground with its droppings. One bat can drop as many as 60,000 seeds in a single night. In this way, bats actually help to regrow the rain forest after it has been cut down. It is not an animal's size that is important, but what it does in the environment.

A keystone species, such as the mountain lion or the shark, may also be considered an **umbrella species.** If an umbrella species is protected, then many other animals are protected at the same time. However, not all umbrella species are keystone species. A keystone species is essential to its environment and all the animals that live in it. Without it, the ecosystem would fall apart. An umbrella species is also important, but its removal does not necessarily cause a serious breakdown in the community. For instance, the spotted owl is an umbrella species in the forests of the American Northwest. Spotted owls need a lot of space to live and hunt. If enough habitat is preserved for the spotted owl, then the other animals that live in the area are automatically protected at the same time.

✦ NATURE'S DEFENSES ✦

All biological communities include **predators** and prey. Predators are animals that hunt and kill other animals for food. (In trophic terms they are secondary, or higher-level, consumers.) **Prey** are animals that are killed by other animals for food. (They are usually primary consumers but may also include some secondary consumers, such as mice or frogs that eat insects and are in turn eaten by other animals.) Predator and prey interactions are nature's way of keeping a healthy balance in the ecosystem.

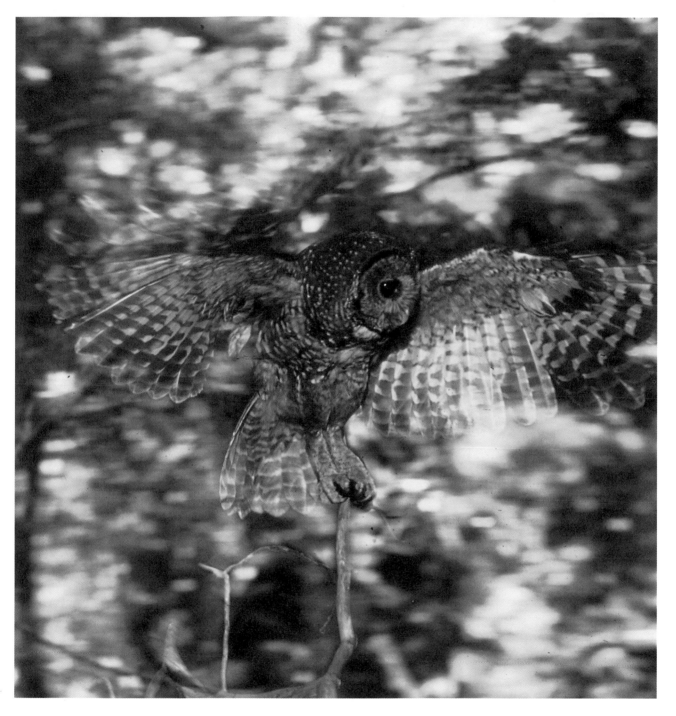

The spotted owl is an endangered species, and its habitats in the Pacific Northwest are protected. Other species living in the same habitats also benefit from the protection.

Predators cannot kill all the prey animals in their community. If they did, they would not have any food to eat in the future. Many prey animals have developed effective ways of escaping from their enemies. Some defenseless creatures are able to survive mainly because they are good at running or swimming or flying away from their enemies. For example, deer and antelope are very fast, running at up to forty miles (64 km) an hour. Many fish and birds can also move quickly. But speed alone is not enough. Some predators can run even faster than many prey. Cheetahs have been seen running as fast as 70 miles (113 km) an hour, faster than the antelope and other prey they hunt. Whales and sharks can swim 25 miles (40 km) an hour, more than twice as fast as minnows, bass, and other small fish. Eagles and falcons have been timed in flight at more than 100 miles (160 km) an hour.

An animal that survives by running away needs more than speed. Some prey animals, therefore, are not only speedy, but they can also dodge and dart about. A rabbit chased by a fox zigzags back and forth to confuse its pursuer. A minnow darts through the water, escaping the jaws of a larger fish. Some animals, such as fleas, frogs, and kangaroos, can escape their enemies by leaping into the air, reaching amazing heights.

Zebras are prey animals that must run for their lives when chased by a predator.

Prey animals may use hiding places to escape from predators. A rabbit or a prairie dog will dive into an underground burrow for safety. Mice and other small rodents may use tall grasses for shelter. Some predators, such as mountain lions, however, may also use tall grasses as a hiding place. A lion will slink through the grasses unseen, ready to pounce on its prey. Before the prey knows what is happening, it is captured.

Some animals have another kind of hiding place—a built-in suit of armor. The turtle's body is covered by an armor-like shell. Normally, the turtle's head, legs, and tail extend from holes in the shell. But at the first sign of danger, its head, legs, and tail suddenly disappear. All that can be seen is a tough, round shell. If a predator turns the turtle over on its back, there is a tough shell underneath as well. Predators usually give up and move on.

Other animals with a suit of armor include clams, oysters, and scallops. These shellfish, or bivalves, have two shells, which have very powerful muscles. They can snap their shells together and keep them so tightly closed that even a strong person cannot open them. Yet some predators do manage to eat bivalves. Sea stars use suction cups on the undersides of their arms to pull a bivalve's shells open. As soon as there is a small gap between the

A clam's shells protect it from many predators, but a sea star can force open the shells and digest the clam's soft insides.

shells, the sea star turns its stomach inside out and inserts it through the gap. It digests the bivalve right inside the shells, then pulls its stomach back inside and sucks up its meal. The oystercatcher is a bird with a long, slim beak. It slips its beak in between an oyster's shells when they are open. Then, using the beak like a long pair of scissors, it quickly cuts the muscle that would snap the oyster shells shut. The sea otter also eats bivalves. This sea mammal uses a tool, such as a flat rock, to open oysters or clams. Floating on its back in the water, the sea otter places the rock on its belly and cracks the bivalve shells.

Sometimes the best way for prey animals to escape from predators is to stay still. Prey that use this method typically have fur, feathers, or skin that matches their surroundings; this acts as camouflage. For instance, a green grasshopper is very hard to pick out among blades of green grass, unless it is hopping about. A crab spider sitting on a flower will change its appearance to the color of the flower. If the flower is pink, the spider will be pink, too. Although this is a useful disguise against predators, it also acts as camouflage when the spider, as a predator itself, waits for an unsuspecting insect prey.

EATING AMMUNITION

Brightly colored frogs in the rain forests of South and Central America are hopping advertisements: "Don't eat me—I'm poisonous!" Species like the poison dart frogs of Colombia make their own poison, batrachotoxin—one of the deadliest poisons in the world.

But other tropical frogs start out as shy, defenseless creatures. They obtain a defense by eating ants, which use poisons called alkaloids to defend themselves and capture prey. The more ants the frogs eat, the more poisonous to predators they become. Scientists found that ants make up nearly three-quarters of the diet of some frogs, which eat hundreds of ants each day. The frogs store the ant alkaloids in special glands in their skin, where they do not harm the frogs.

A child learns very early that a meeting with a buzzing bee can be a very painful experience. Birds that live on insects quickly learn to leave wasps and bees alone. The insects' bright-colored bodies are warning signals in the world of nature. A bee will leave a very painful memory with any predator that bothers it.

Other insects also use their colorful markings to warn predators. There are two kinds of orange and black butterflies that taste so bad that no bird wants to eat them. However, there are also many other orange and black butterflies that do not taste bad. Birds usually leave all of them alone because they cannot tell the difference.

Some animals defend themselves by a kind of chemical warfare. A skunk's black-and-white marking usually acts as a warning to stay away. But if the skunk is threatened, it does not need to run; it will lift its tail to the predator and spray out an extremely bad-smelling chemical, which lingers long after the skunk is gone. It usually takes only one encounter for an animal to learn to leave skunks alone. Some insects also use bad-smelling or stinging sprays as a chemical defense.

Nature's defenses are helpful to many animals. Even the individual animals that fall victim to predators may help to teach the predators to recognize nature's warning signals and thus actually help to keep their whole species alive.

✦ POPULATION EXPLOSIONS ✦

The predator/prey relationships are usually fairly successful in keeping a balance in biological communities. But sometimes certain species go through population cycles when the ecosystem is thrown out of balance. This occurs when animals reproduce so effectively that they do not have enough food or living space. Meanwhile, their population explosion affects other links in the food chains of their community, producing changes that eventually bring things back into balance.

The number of snowshoe rabbits, for example, varies over a cycle of about nine or ten years. Gradually the population builds up from year to year until enormous numbers are reached. In one area in Canada, it was estimated that the snowshoe rabbit population was once as high as 5,000 per square mile. Then suddenly, the population dropped, without any warning, to about a tenth of what it had been the year before. Apparently, some predators, such as lynxes, great horned owls, and goshawks, have population cycles of their own, which follow the nine- or ten-year cycle of the snowshoe rabbit. As the prey population increases, so does the predator population. As the predators feed on the snowshoe rabbit and reduce its numbers, many of them starve to death because of lack of prey, and so they experience their own population crash.

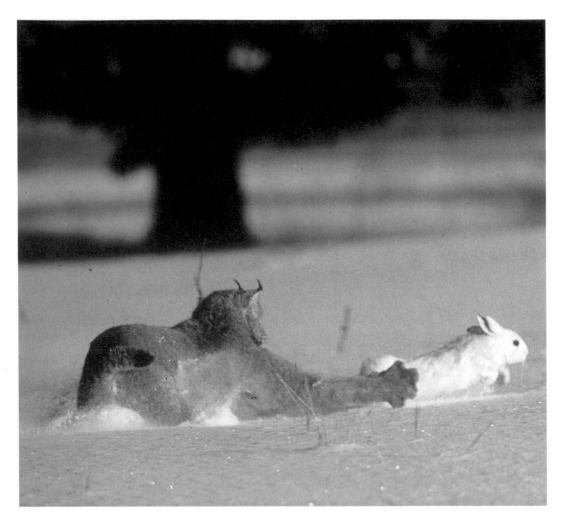

A lynx reaches for its favorite food, a snowshoe rabbit. The population cycles of both animals are closely tied together and undergo changes to maintain a balance between predator and prey.

These population explosions have a serious impact on the food chains. For example, as the number of snowshoe rabbits grows, the amount of plants eaten greatly increases. But there is only so much plant food in one area. Eventually, the rabbits have eaten it all, cutting down the food supply for future generations.

Scientists have discovered another factor that helps to limit runaway animal populations. For instance, the snowshoe rabbit's liver, which normally stores an animal starch called glycogen, does not work properly when the rabbit experiences stress from overcrowding. Glycogen is easily changed to glucose, the sugar that animals use for a source of energy. When snowshoe rabbits are overcrowded, their livers do not store as much glycogen as usual. Instead of running away from predators, the rabbits with damaged livers lack energy and may lie down and die before the predator has even reached them.

After the population crash, the few survivors find themselves in a world with plenty of room and plenty of food. Soon the predator population is in balance with the prey population, and gradually they build up their numbers again.

FOOD ENERGY IN PYRAMIDS

In the early 1920s the English ecologist Charles S. Elton spent a summer studying the feeding habits of foxes on an arctic island. He counted all the small animals and birds that were eaten by a fox, and the insects and worms that were eaten by the small animals. He noticed that the total numbers of the different animals formed a pyramid. As the food chain rose from the producers to the primary, secondary, and tertiary consumers, the number of organisms decreased. The producers were at the bottom of the pyramid, which consisted of millions of plants. The second level of the pyramid included the primary consumers, which consisted of thousands of insects and worms. The third level of the pyramid included the secondary producers, which consisted of hundreds of small animals. The fox was at the fourth level, which included the tertiary consumers and had the smallest number of organisms.

Today, feeding relationships among organisms at different trophic levels can be illustrated in what is known as **ecological pyramids.** They are also sometimes called Eltonian pyramids, in honor of the importance of Elton's contributions to the science of ecology.

✦ THE PYRAMID OF NUMBERS ✦

The pyramid-shaped relationship among the number of organisms at each trophic level is known as a **pyramid of numbers.** This kind of pyramid arrangement worked well for the ecosystem Elton studied, but in some cases, the numbers of organisms do not form such a neat pyramid. In a redwood forest, for example, a few trees could provide food for huge numbers of insects, which in turn would support smaller numbers of birds and other carnivores. The upper levels of the pyramid of numbers would thus show the usual shape, but the base—instead of being the largest—would be small. The trophic relationships could be described more accurately by considering the organisms in terms of their weight, rather than of their numbers.

✦ THE PYRAMID OF BIOMASS ✦

At first, Elton thought that the total weight of the organisms at any one level of the pyramid would be equal to the weight of those at any other level. A fox, for example, weighs much more than the individual rabbits, mice, and birds that it eats, but it eats so many of them that their total weight is substantial. However, when Elton calculated the weight, or **biomass,** of all the organisms at each level, he was surprised to find that they were not equal. The biomass also decreased with each step up the trophic levels—so there was also a **pyramid of biomass.** The fox ate much more than its own weight of rabbits, mice, and birds. They, in turn, consumed more than their own weight in insects, seeds, and other foods; and the insects ate more than their own weight in plant food.

What happens to the biomass that is lost from one level to the next higher one? When a fox eats a rabbit, for instance, it does not eat the rabbit's entire body. It may eat only the meat, leaving the skin and bones. Part of the meat consumed may not be digested and leaves the fox's body as waste products. The wastes and leftovers are then eaten by scavengers. Part of the food eaten goes to build biomass for the growing fox. Another part is used for energy for the animal's activities, such as moving, breathing, digesting, and reproducing. Thus, only a small part of the rabbit's biomass is actually converted to fox biomass.

✦ THE PYRAMID OF ENERGY ✦

If we think of the organisms at each trophic level in terms of the energy they contain rather than their weight, we find that the energy relationships form a **pyramid of energy.** This pyramid demonstrates why a large biomass of little animals supports a smaller biomass of big animals.

All living things get energy from food. The energy stored in foods is mea-

Each level of this energy pyramid represents the amount of energy stored at that level. At the base are the producers where most of the energy from the sun is stored. The other levels represent consumers. Each level contains less energy than the one below it.

sured in units called **calories.** A calorie is the amount of heat needed to raise the temperature of one gram of water by one degree centigrade. (The "calorie" used as a measure of foods' energy content is actually a kilocalorie—1,000 calories.) When a fox eats a rabbit, food energy from the rabbit is transferred and stored in the fox's body. But when the fox uses energy to run, for instance, a lot of the energy is lost as heat.

Since organisms use up energy when they move, reproduce, eliminate wastes, and grow, they cannot pass on all the energy they have eaten in the form of food. In fact, studies of various ecosystems indicated that in general, only about 10 percent of the energy in any trophic level is transferred to organisms in the next higher trophic level. This is called the "10 percent rule." For example, to gain one pound (0.45 kg), a person would have to eat about 10 pounds (4.5 kg) of bass; the bass would need to eat 100 pounds (45 kg) of minnows; the minnows would need 1,000 pounds (450 kg) of water fleas; and the water fleas would need to feed on 10,000 pounds (4,500 kg) of algae. More recent studies have shown, however, that the 10 percent rule is not always an accurate guide to the transfer of energy in nature. Instead, in real-life food webs the efficiency of energy transfer may be as low as 0.05 percent or as high as 20 percent.

PICKY EATERS

Most people would be afraid if a great white shark swam past them in the ocean. Recent studies, however, have shown that the great white shark is actually a picky eater and does not really live up to its man-eating reputation. According to Dr. A. Peter Klimley, a biologist at the University of California Bodega Marine Laboratory, great white sharks prefer to feed on animals such as seals and whales, which contain energy-rich layers of fat. Humans and sea otters are too lean. Fat has more than twice the energy value of muscle. Since great white sharks have very slow digestion, they are less likely to waste their time feeding on anything that does not give them the energy they need in a short amount of time.

Only a small amount of energy gets passed on to other trophic levels, so there are usually no more than four or five links in a food chain. At the bottom of the food web are the producers, the largest population group. Next come the primary consumers, which must eat large numbers of producers to get enough energy to function and grow. Going up each level of the pyramid, less and less energy is available, and the number of organisms it can support is smaller. This explains why there are typically more prey than predators in a community.

Thus, the pyramid of numbers, the pyramid of biomass, and the pyramid of energy all describe relationships among organisms in a single ecosystem.

How Nature Recycles

What materials does your community recycle? Newspapers, glass bottles, aluminum cans, plastics? We tend to think of recycling programs as something developed rather recently, when people became aware of the problems our "throwaway society" was creating for the environment. Actually, though, recycling has always been a part of our world. Some of the air molecules you breathe may have passed through the lungs of Caesar or Shakespeare or some other famous person of the past. Some of the calcium in your bones may once have been a part of a dinosaur's skeleton or the shell of some ancient sea creature.

All living things need certain chemical elements, or essential nutrients, to grow and maintain themselves properly. These nutrients can be found in the soil, the water, or the atmosphere. Energy from the sun flows through ecosystems on earth, passes from one trophic level to the next, and disappears in the environment in the process. But the earth does not receive a continuous supply of chemical elements from anywhere. They cannot be produced or used up but are passed around from the environment to living organisms and back again. The same essential nutrients must be used over and over. This kind of nutrient recycling, which usually involves both living things and the earth, is known as a **biogeochemical cycle,** from *bio,* meaning "living" and *geo,* meaning "earth."

All nutrients in an ecosystem must go through biogeochemical cycles. These cycles and the food chains are linked together in many complex ways. For instance, plants take carbon dioxide from the air and water and minerals from the soil, and using energy from the sun, they make food through photosynthesis. The animals that feed on the plants use some of the nutrients for growth, daily activities, and reproduction. The plant materials that cannot be used by the animals are eliminated as waste products, the elements of which are returned to the environment by decomposers. Animals that eat other animals in turn use some of the nutrients for their own growth, daily activities, and reproduction. When the plants and animals die, decomposers break down the organic material and return the nutrients to the soil and air. Thus, most of the food produced by plants is eventually broken down into carbon dioxide, water, and minerals and returned to the ecosystem for reuse by other living things.

These logs will eventually decay and return to the soil, thanks to decomposers such as the slime mold covering them.

✦ THE WATER CYCLE ✦

Probably the most familiar and visible biogeochemical cycle is the water cycle. Water evaporates from the surface of rivers and streams, lakes and oceans. When weather conditions are right, the water vapor in the clouds can condense into liquid water, which falls to the surface as rain. Some of the rainwater then falls on land areas and drains off into streams, rivers, and eventually into the ocean.

Some of the rain is absorbed by the soil and drawn up through the roots of plants. Water pressure in the stems and leaves helps to keep plants sturdy—it is the only "skeleton" that some plants have. But plants continually lose water through tiny openings in their leaves, so they need a new supply. (If you forget to water a houseplant in a pot, it soon droops and wilts.)

Animals (including humans) are another important part of nature's water cycle. They drink water and also take in moisture in juicy fruits and leaves of plants. Your own body is really about two-thirds water. Animals lose some of their body water when they get rid of their body wastes, and there is water vapor in the breath they exhale. When an animal dies, the rest of its body water is returned to the cycle.

✦ THE NITROGEN CYCLE ✦

Nature also recycles important chemical elements. Nitrogen, for example, is a gas that makes up 78 percent of the earth's atmosphere. Most plants and animals cannot use pure nitrogen gas, yet it is a part of many important body chemicals. A key link in the nitrogen cycle is played by specialized bacteria that live in the soil or in plant roots. These **nitrogen fixers** change nitrogen gas into chemical forms that plants can use. The plants further change these simple nitrogen compounds into proteins and other complex substances. Animals get the nitrogen compounds they need by eating plants or other animals.

When animals and plants die, decay bacteria break down the complex nitrogen compounds in their bodies into simpler substances, such as water and the strong-smelling gas ammonia. Other bacteria carry the process further to produce nitrogen gas. This is the reverse of the nitrogen-fixing chemical reactions, and it completes the cycle, returning nitrogen to the atmosphere.

The natural nitrogen cycle is perfectly balanced— the nitrogen removed from the soil by plants and

> DID YOU KNOW?
>
> The air over a single acre (0.4 hectare) of land contains about 35,000 tons of nitrogen.

animals is completely replaced by the nitrogen-fixing bacteria and the decay processes.

✦ THE OXYGEN CYCLE ✦

Living animals and plants play key roles in the recycling of another important element, oxygen. Although this gas makes up close to 21 percent of the earth's atmosphere, scientists believe that there was practically none of it in the air when our planet was first formed. At that time, billions of years ago, the earth's oxygen was mainly bound up in chemical compounds, in the water of the oceans and in rocks and minerals. For the first living things, oxygen was a deadly poison. But gradually creatures appeared that could make oxygen less poisonous or even use it to generate energy.

Eventually there were plants that not only used oxygen but also produced it. During photosynthesis, as plants use sunlight energy to combine carbon dioxide and water into food materials, oxygen gas is released as a by-product. All the oxygen in the earth's atmosphere was formed by plants and photosynthesizing microorganisms. The microscopic algae that float on the ocean's surface in our present-day world, as well as trees, grasses, and other land plants, help to supply oxygen to the atmosphere.

Animals cannot produce oxygen, but they are heavy consumers of this important gas. They use it in **respiration,** a process somewhat like a fire burning, in which complex chemicals are combined with oxygen to release energy. Land animals obtain the oxygen they need by breathing air. Water dwellers use the oxygen dissolved in the water. Plants "breathe," too, but the amount of oxygen their respiration uses up is generally far smaller than the amount they produce in photosynthesis. So in the natural oxygen cycle, plants add oxygen to the atmosphere, while animals use it up.

✦ THE CARBON CYCLE ✦

The carbon cycle is interlocked with the oxygen cycle. The connecting link between these two cycles is carbon dioxide, which is formed when the carbon compounds combine with oxygen—either in a burning fire or in respiration. Proteins, sugars, fats, and many other complex substances that are found in the bodies of plants and animals all contain carbon. This element is also a major part of the fossil fuels: coal, oil, and gas, which were formed from the remains of ancient plant and animal life.

Fish get oxygen from the water through their gills, which appear in this photo as slits on the side of the shark.

There is not much carbon dioxide in the earth's atmosphere, compared to the amount of nitrogen and oxygen—only 0.035 percent. But this gas is very important for living things. It is the main raw material of photosynthesis: Thus, it is the ultimate source of all food for our planet's creatures.

Carbon dioxide from the atmosphere may be carried down into streams and rivers by the rain, or it may dissolve directly into the surface waters of lakes and oceans. (The earth's oceans contain sixty times as much carbon dioxide as there is in the atmosphere.) The tiny plants that float on the ocean surface in huge numbers use some of the dissolved carbon dioxide in photosynthesis and play a major role in producing oxygen gas. But some of these microscopic creatures use carbon dioxide in forming hard protective shells around their delicate bodies. When they die, they sink to the bottom, taking some of the carbon out of circulation.

Animals and plants that build carbon into their body chemicals also take this element out of circulation—at least temporarily. But when they die and their bodies are broken down, the carbon they contained is recycled. Carbon compounds in rocks may also be returned to circulation when they are dissolved out by rainwater or vaporized by erupting volcanoes.

✦ THE PHOSPHORUS CYCLE ✦

Many mineral elements from the soil are important for living organisms. They are taken in by plants and pass up the food chains to animals. One of the most important of these minerals is the chemical element phosphorus. This element is a key part of DNA and RNA, the chemicals of heredity. Phosphorus is also part of a compound called **ATP,** which living things use to store the energy they need to keep handy for the work that goes on constantly inside their cells.

Phosphorus is found in rocks in compounds called phosphates, in which it is linked with oxygen. Rain that soaks into the soil dissolves out some of the phosphates from the bits of rock. Plant roots take in dissolved phosphates together with the water they absorb. The plants build phosphorus into their chemicals, and it then is passed on to the animals that eat the plants. Decomposers working on the body wastes of living organisms and the bodies of dead ones return phosphorus to the soil.

Phosphorus recycling does not work perfectly, however. Some of the phosphates returned to the soil are carried by rainwater into streams and rivers and eventually washed away to sea, where they form hard rocky deposits on the ocean bottom. Sewage-disposal systems built by humans carry phosphorus-rich wastes directly into the earth's water systems. Not only body wastes but also detergents used to wash clothes and dishes contain phosphorus. About 3.5 million tons of phosphorus are carried away by the rivers each year. Not all of this is lost, though. Some of the phosphorus that washes into the ocean is taken up by phytoplankton, the tiny single-celled plantlike organisms that live in the surface waters, and passes up the ocean food chains as the phytoplankton are eaten by tiny animals, which are prey for larger sea dwellers. Some of the phosphorus is returned to the land in the bodies of fish caught for food and in small amounts in bird droppings, or guano.

Various other minerals are also needed by living organisms. In some cases the amounts needed are so small they can barely be measured, yet they are essential for health and life. The food chains help to distribute them among the earth's creatures and eventually return them to the environment. All the biogeo-chemical cycles are connected to one another and are vital to all living things on earth. The constant recycling of nutrients makes it possible for ecosystems to exist over extremely long periods of time.

SIX

INVADERS IN THE FOOD CHAIN

What happens when a toxic substance or a foreign species invades an ecosystem? Just one tiny change in an environment can result in a series of chain reactions, in which the food chains play a major role.

Take the case of DDT, for example. This pesticide was considered a miracle when it was introduced in the 1940s. In less developed countries, especially in the tropics, it saved the lives of millions of people by killing the mosquitoes that spread malaria. Larger crop production resulted from DDT's destruction of insect pests, and the increased food supply saved even more people from starvation. DDT was so powerful and long-lasting that only one application was needed. People were not yet aware of the damaging effects this "amazing" pesticide was going to have on the complex web of life.

In the mid 1950s, the World Health Organization sprayed DDT on the island of Borneo to eliminate malaria. Soon side effects of DDT started to appear. DDT killed not only the mosquitoes but also other insects, such as flies and cockroaches, that lived in the people's houses. Caterpillars that fed on the thatched roofs of woven leaves and straw were unaffected by the pesticide. The wasps that normally preyed on the caterpillars were killed, however. When the wasps were no longer present, the caterpillar population soon rose out of control and caused the roofs to collapse.

Gecko lizards also lived in the houses and ate the dead bodies of the flies and cockroaches. Since DDT cannot be broken down and tends to accumulate in the fatty tissues of organisms, geckos died from the poison concentrated in the insect bodies. Village cats fed on the gecko lizards and also died from DDT poisoning. Once the cats were eliminated, the rat population overran the island. Fleas that lived on the rats were carriers of a disease called sylvatic plague, which could be transmitted to humans. New cats were then flown to different parts of the island to reduce the rat population and help bring things back to normal.

Ecologists often use ecological pyramids to illustrate how toxic chemicals in the environment can gradually accumulate in the bodies of the organisms in an ecosystem. This effect, known as **bioconcentration,** explains how a toxic chemical may build to a level high enough to kill the organism. Bioconcentration may also lead to **biological magnification,** the increasing concentration of a toxin as it moves up the trophic levels of a food chain.

For instance, when DDT was widely used, runoff from fields contaminated streams, rivers, and oceans with DDT. The algae growing in these waters absorbed the DDT. When tiny aquatic animals ate the algae, the DDT was passed along the food chain. Larger fish ate these poisoned smaller fish, and DDT accumulated in their bodies.

Crops were regularly dusted with DDT before its danger to the environment was known. DDT contamination affected many food chains.

At each higher trophic level, the concentration of DDT increased. When a large fish ate many small fish contaminated with DDT, a huge dose of DDT accumulated in the large fish's body because of the number of poisoned fish it had eaten. When birds ate the larger fish, the DDT was concentrated further. It did not kill the birds directly, but it reduced the amount of calcium in the shells of eggs the female birds laid. The eggshells were so weak that they broke when the parent birds sat on them.

A number of bird species, including peregrine falcons, ospreys, brown pelicans, American eagles, and the California condor, lost whole generations of chicks and were in danger of becoming extinct. DDT is so persistent in the environment that long after it was banned in the United States in 1972, birds continued to lay contaminated eggs.

UNEXPECTED POISONS

In the 1930s Midwesterners were alarmed when their valued lake trout began disappearing from the Great Lakes. It was believed that the sea lamprey, which looks like an eel and preys on lake trout, was responsible for the decline of the fish population. Biologists then released chemicals that would reduce the lamprey population and were thought to be harmless to the rest of the marine life. Recent studies, however, suggest that the lake trout may have been poisoned. Scientists noticed that the lake trout's dramatic decline started about the same time that large amounts of dioxins, polychlorinated biphenyls (PCBs), and other chemicals were poured into the lake.

In 1992 scientists had evidence suggesting that lake trout embryos exposed to dioxins could develop a deadly disease called blue sac syndrome and that future generations would not survive. Although restocking dioxin-free lake trout in the Great Lakes has produced some improvement in the population, recent laboratory tests indicate that less-than-lethal amounts of dioxin-like pollutants may still cause harm to the fish. In 1995 the EPA established limits on discharges of some 40 toxic chemicals, including DDT and PCBs, into the Great Lakes.

Lake trout are very important in the food web. They are one of the top predators in the Great Lakes and keep the numbers of the smaller fish under control. As the lake trout disappeared, other fish have overrun the waters and have begun a chain reaction among other species in the aquatic ecosystem.

✦ HORMONE POLLUTANTS ✦

In the early 1990s British biologists noticed something strange about the fish they had taken out of the sewage-filled River Lee near London—the reproductive organs of the males, the testes, were covered with eggs. But eggs are normally produced by females in their reproductive organs, the ovaries. Scientists believed that something in the water was acting as a sex hormone and was interfering with reproductive development. Two studies on this phenomenon were conducted. A study sponsored by the U.S. Geological Survey showed that fish living in streams in the United States also appear to have unusual levels of sex hormones. In another survey British researchers suggested that it is not industrial chemicals that are disrupting the fishes' reproductive development; natural hormones, **estrogens,** in women's urine may be responsible. In addition, both studies seemed to show that the fish found in polluted waters were more likely to have abnormal levels of hormones than those found in cleaner waters.

In a more intensive study at sewage-contaminated waters of Lake Mead near Las Vegas, Nevada, the researchers also found that the male fish had unusually high levels of vitellogenin, a protein involved in egg-laying that normally occurs only in females. In another study, sponsored by the U.K. Environment Agency, British researchers collected sewage from three treatment plants and managed to isolate the compounds that were likely to act like estrogens in the fish. The researchers discovered that these compounds were not industrial chemicals but were three hormones found in women—17B-estradiol, estrone, and ethynyl estradiol. This last one, which was found in small amounts, is a strong synthetic hormone in birth-control pills.

WASH WHAT YOU EAT

Pesticides are still one of the most effective weapons to fight insect pests in crops. Residues from pesticide sprays may remain on the outer surface of crops after harvesting. Therefore, it is a good idea to wash or peel fruits and vegetables before eating them because the accumulation of these pesticide residues can be harmful to us.

These concentrations of hormone pollutants increase as they move up the food chain. The Florida panther, for instance, consumes a strong dose of the hormone pollutants when it feeds on raccoons that eat the contaminated fish. Some scientists believe that this contamination has been responsible for various reproductive problems in Florida panthers. Other species, such as alligators, have also experienced the effects of hormone pollutants. In 1980, there was an accidental spill of dicofol, a pesticide, in Lake Apopka in Florida—the home of many alligators. Scientists believe that this hormonelike pollutant damages the reproductive systems of alligators. As a result, there has been a 90 percent reduction in the number of young alligators in the lake.

Hormone pollutants, which can affect reproductive systems, have reduced the number of young alligators in Florida's Lake Apopka.

✦ ANIMAL INVADERS ✦

People are becoming more and more aware of the dangerous effects that pesticides and other pollutants have on wildlife and humans. Deeply wanting to find a safe way to eliminate pests without harming other living things, biologists have tried to take a more natural route—fighting nature with nature. Scientists call this **biological pest control.** Instead of using chemicals, they bring in foreign species that prey on certain pests and let nature take its course.

For instance, an Australian tree called the melaleuca, which lives in the Florida Everglades, is spreading through the forests at a rate of 35 to 50 acres (14 to 20 hectares) a day. The melaleuca has become an environmental hazard, forcing out the native plants and causing problems for the electrical equipment and power lines. In May 1997 the U.S. Department of Agriculture released snout beetles imported from Australia into the Florida Everglades to control the melaleuca's growth. The snout beetle eats only the melaleuca and prefers the tree's new leaves and flower buds. Scientists hope this will keep the melaleuca from spreading.

Similar biological control efforts have been successful, but there have also been some disasters. For example, in the 1930s the poisonous cane toad was brought into Australia to get rid of a beetle that was destroying sugarcane crops. However, the beetles fly only at night, and the toads, which are active during the day, were unable to eat them. The toads started to invade the land, and 102 toads became a trillion.

Bringing a strange species into a new habitat is always a risk. It seems that no matter how familiar scientists become with an ecosystem, it is hard to predict what will happen when a foreign species is released into it.

In biological pest control, scientists can control what species are introduced into a habitat, but they cannot control the effects. Sometimes animals invade habitats without planning—and the effects on the environment can be disastrous.

Scientists think that many animals invade new ecosystems by stowing away in a ship's ballast water. Ballast water is used to stabilize cargo ships. When the water is pumped into a ship, it carries many different organisms. The organisms are then released into new surroundings when the ship docks and dumps the ballast water.

When an animal or plant invades new territories, it can cause serious problems for the environment and the species living in it. Consider the European green crab. It has lived in the waters off the eastern shores of North America for about 180 years. By the late 1980s the crab had made its way to the West Coast, where it was found in San Francisco Bay. It is probable that the crab came to San Francisco in ballast water or in bait shipments. The green crab has an insatiable appetite and feeds on oysters, clams, and other crab species. It is not only threatening the commercial shellfisheries in the Pacific Northwest, but it may have disastrous effects on the food chain as well. Scientists are concerned that birds may have to compete with the green crabs for food and that this may result in a decline in the bird population.

✦ SEVEN ✦

HUMANS AND FOOD CHAINS

During the 1950s and the 1960s, aboveground nuclear-weapons testing took place at the Nevada Test Site, north of Las Vegas. The test explosions released many radioactive substances into the environment, including dangerous isotopes of strontium, cesium, and iodine. Cows that ate grass or drank water on which these radioisotopes fell secreted some of the radioactive materials in their milk. Researchers at the National Cancer Institute now believe that people who lived in the area during that time may have been exposed to radioactive iodine when they drank contaminated milk. The amount of iodine exposure during the test period was about two **rads** (a unit of radiation), which is five times the amount of radiation a woman gets from a mammogram today.

Some researchers think that between 10,000 and 75,000 children who were exposed to the radioactive iodine fallout may develop thyroid cancer sometime during their lives. Others feel that since thyroid tumors associated with radiation overdose usually show up within about twenty-five years, cancers caused by the Nevada tests probably would have appeared by now.

Whenever foreign chemicals or poisons enter the environment, they eventually make their way up the food chains and may affect people's lives. Humans are especially vulnerable because we are at the top of the food chains, and toxic pollutants usually become more concentrated as they pass up the trophic levels.

This crater, wider than the length of three football fields, resulted from a nuclear test in 1962. It is not certain just how much radiation from aboveground nuclear testing has crept into food chains.

✦ POLLUTANTS IN THE FOOD CHAIN ✦

Pollution in the environment is an ongoing problem. Health scientists are especially concerned these days about people who eat contaminated fish. Research has shown that the PCBs and other hormone pollutants that are found in many Great Lakes fish have damaged the development of infants and children whose mothers ate these fish. Women who eat contaminated fish may pass the pollutants on to their children before birth and through breastfeeding. Studies have shown that there may be a link between high doses of PCBs in a woman's breast milk and behavioral problems in her newborn.

At Wayne State University in Detroit, Michigan, Sandra and Joseph Jacobson found that pregnant women who ate large amounts of Lake Michigan fish gave birth to babies with lower weight and smaller head circumference than the babies of women who did not eat the fish. Also, the babies whose mothers had the highest levels of PCBs in their blood later scored the lowest on intelligence testing, which included verbal and memory tests. In addition, recent studies at the State University of New York at Oswego found that the newborns of mothers who had eaten Lake Ontario fish had more abnormal reflexes and took longer to calm down after being startled.

Other studies also may suggest an influence of hormonelike pollutants on humans. A 1996 analysis of sperm-count studies in twenty countries seemed to indicate that men are becoming less fertile. This could be the result of an accumulation of pollutants, with effects similar to those of female hormones, taken in through the food chain. However, sperm counts did not decline everywhere. Regional differences in pollution or other factors might be responsible for these findings.

BEWARE OF RAW SHELLFISH

Mollusks, which include shellfish like oysters, clams, and mussels, may be a delicacy for some people, but they may also make people sick if they are eaten raw. Since mollusks cannot move, they eat by filtering water through their bodies, removing nutrients in the process. Unfortunately, they can also take in and store harmful bacteria and viruses that can cause a variety of illnesses. These come from human sewage that contaminates the waters where the mollusks live. When people eat contaminated shellfish raw, they also consume the viruses and bacteria.

It is not clear if these hormonelike pollutants are a problem for society as a whole or are just isolated cases. More research is needed, but some international organizations agree that there is a problem and that exposure to pollutants should be limited. Members of the United Nations Economic Commission for Europe (which includes the United States and Canada) are trying to prepare a plan that would eliminate the use of twelve persistent pollutants. Donella Meadows, a researcher at Dartmouth College, believes more pollutants should be thoroughly tested. Only a fraction of the tens of thousands of chemicals dumped into the environment each year have been tested for basic toxicity. "Chemicals aren't like people; they should be assumed guilty until proven innocent," Meadows asserts.

✦ MAINTAINING A BALANCE ✦

For millions of years, nature has somehow maintained a balance among all living things. Predator and prey relationships in the wild usually keep the animal populations in check. But the human population continues to grow, and so does the amount of food people consume. Many scientists believe that humans are eating more than they need, and that there may not be enough food for everyone. They predict that as the number of people on earth continues to increase, eventually even people in the wealthy nations will not be able to afford to eat much meat. We may all have to feed lower on the food chains, depending more on grains, vegetables, and fruits for our food energy.

> **DID YOU KNOW?**
>
> The average American adult eats more than half a ton of food each year—and an estimated 20 to 25 percent of Americans weigh at least 20 percent more than they should.

Such a change in diet may not be a bad thing. For years, health experts have been saying we should eat more plant foods and less fat, especially the saturated fat that is found in meat. For many Americans, this would be a dramatic and difficult change in eating habits, but for some people a diet without meat is already a way of life. These people are called **vegetarians.**

There are several different kinds of vegetarians. **Semi-vegetarians** eat dairy foods, eggs, chicken, and fish, but no other animal flesh. **Pesco-vegetarians** eat dairy foods, eggs, and fish, but no other animal flesh. There are also **lacto-ovo-vegetarians,** who eat dairy foods and eggs but no other animal flesh; **lacto-vegetarians,** who eat dairy products but no eggs; and **ovo-vegetarians,** who eat eggs but no dairy foods or animal flesh. Finally, the **vegans** do not eat any animal foods of any kind. In some parts of the world, vegetarian diets are a cultural tradition—or a necessity if little meat (or money to buy it) is available. A number of people in wealthier nations choose vegetarianism for ethical reasons, because they do not want to be responsible for the killing of animals.

Some health experts believe that vegetarians may be healthier than people who eat animal products. Studies strongly suggest that vegetarians have a lower

A selection of foods for a vegetarian diet

risk of obesity, hypertension, and heart disease. Certain studies indicate that vegetarians may also have a lower risk of colon cancer.

Many vegetarians think they are doing their body good by eliminating fatty meats from their diet and eating only plant foods. A vegetarian diet may not completely fulfill a person's nutritional needs, however. Vegans, the strictest vegetarians, run the greatest risk of nutritional deficiencies. People who eat only plant foods must eat larger amounts of food to get the same amount of energy as a person who eats animal foods. Remember that the energy yield decreases by about 90 percent with each level in the food chain. Moreover, humans use plant foods much less efficiently than do natural herbivores. Our bodies cannot get nourishment from the cellulose found in plants the way animals like cows can. A cow's stomach contains helpful bacteria that break down the cellulose in the grass that the cow eats. That is why a cow can get more nutritional value from plants than we can. Since humans cannot digest cellulose, plant fibers just pass out with our body wastes, without providing us with any food energy.

TAKE A BITE

Most humans are omnivores. We eat both animal and plant foods. In fact, our long-ago ancestors adapted to an omnivorous diet; our teeth are evidence of this. We can eat a wider variety of foods than most other animals because we have four different kinds of teeth. The sharp, chisel-shaped incisors in the front act like knives to slice and bite off chunks of food. They work like the incisors that herbivores use to clip off grass or other plant leaves. Next to the incisors are the canines. Like the slashing fangs of carnivores, our pointed canines are used to tear food into bits. Next come the premolars, double-pointed teeth that work like the blades of scissors to cut food. They also help the molars, broad teeth with raised bumps and ridges, to crush and grind food into a smooth pulp, the way the premolars and molars of herbivores grind up grains and plant fibers.

It is hard for vegetarians to get enough of certain vitamins that are plentiful in animal foods but not in plants. Vegetarians may also not get enough protein. Food proteins are digested into smaller molecules called **amino acids,** which are then used as building blocks to make the thousands of proteins we need for growth, repair, and the many activities of our individual cells. Our bodies can make some amino acids from sugars and other nutrients, but there are others that we need for building proteins but cannot make on our own. We have to get these **essential amino acids** from foods.

Most animal foods, such as meat, poultry, fish, eggs, cheese, and milk, contain all the essential amino acids. The food proteins from these animal sources are called complete proteins. A few kinds of plant proteins are complete, too. Soybean products such as tofu have proteins that are very much like animal proteins and contain all the essential amino acids.

Most plant proteins, however, are not complete. They contain only small amounts of one or more essential amino acids. The proteins in foods such as legumes (beans and peas), nuts, seeds, grains, and vegetables are all incomplete proteins. Just one of these foods cannot supply all our protein needs by itself, but certain combinations of plant foods—such as rice and beans—can together supply all the essential amino acids. To eat a healthy, balanced diet, vegetarians must be especially careful to eat a variety of foods. The more varied the diet, nutrition experts advise, the better the chances of getting all the nutrients we need.

As for the rest of us—moderation is the key. Meat in the diet can be healthy and nutritious, but overconsumption can cause problems.

✦ LEARNING FOR THE FUTURE ✦

We have seen how pollution can have serious effects on the food chain. Ecologists are trying to think of ways to eliminate pollutants in the ecosystem. In November 1996 ecologist George Chan began a very interesting experiment on the largest island of Fiji, in the South Pacific. Chan is a strong supporter of **integrated farming,** which uses the waste products of one agricultural industry as

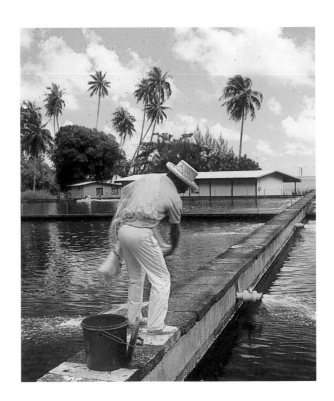

Fish farming and other controlled environments for raising food may be one way to eliminate pollutants from the ecosystem. The farm shown here produces prawns.

fertilizer or fuel for another, which in turn will add little or no pollution to the environment. He is working with the help of students from the Montfort Boys' Town, a boys' school on the island.

Fiji has an established fish-farming industry, but fishing is in jeopardy because of brewery waste dumping—more than 14 million cubic feet (400,000 cubic meters) each year. The brewery waste has covered some of the coral reefs and destroyed much of the local sea life. Moreover, many Fiji residents eat fish contaminated by the harmful waste. To combat this problem, Chan plans to use the waste as fertilizer for mushrooms. As the mushrooms grow, they produce a residue. Normally, this residue is dumped on fields, where it fertilizes crops but may also cause an overflow of muck. At Montfort, however, the residue will be used as food for chickens, pigs, and other animals. Since it is both nutritious and safe, it makes an excellent slop, or feed.

Animal wastes are then put into a contraption called the "decomposer," where the chemicals in the wastes separate. During this process, methane gas is released and collected in a compartment at the top of the device, while the solid or liquid wastes settle to the bottom. Usually, the methane would be released into the atmosphere and lost. But in the Fiji project, it will be bottled and used to operate a gas generator to power the lights of the school, or it will be sold.

Meanwhile, the solid matter left in the decomposer goes through a process that gets rid of some of its bacteria at each stage, eliminating some of its potential to cause illnesses. The decontaminated manure is then converted into nutrients like nitrogen, phosphorus, and potash, which are normally used as fertilizer for farming. It is then put into several cleansing ponds, where bacteria, plankton, and other micro-scavengers will eat all the unwanted, leftover parts of the original animal wastes. In the final stage, this matter becomes food for the farmed fish.

The nutrients in the fish pond water will be used for growing flowers, strawberries, and vegetables floating on top of the pond, reducing the amount of muck left for disposal. The produce will be harvested for public consumption, leaving little or no waste at the farm. Chan's integrated farming should be very productive for the Montfort Boys' Town; it will require less money than traditional farming and will bring income to the poor town. Meanwhile, the project will help to clean up the coral reefs.

There is much that the world at large can learn from this small experiment in applied ecology. A thorough, in-depth study of the complex ways our planet's living organisms are linked together in food chains and webs can provide insights into how humans can live in harmony with our world, providing for our own needs while preserving resources for future generations.

GLOSSARY

alkaloids—poisonous chemicals made by some plants, ants, and other organisms.

amino acids—the chemical building blocks of proteins.

antenna pigments—chlorophyll and other pigment molecules in a photosystem that gather light energy.

ATP—adenosine triphosphate: a chemical compound used by living organisms for the temporary storage of energy.

autotrophs—producers; the basis of all food chains, which produce food by photosynthesis or chemosynthesis.

batrachotoxin—a deadly poison made by the poison dart frogs of Colombia.

bioconcentration—the accumulation of high concentrations of poisons or other chemicals from foods in the bodies of animals that eat them.

biodiversity—the variety of species at each trophic level in an ecosystem.

biogeochemical cycle—recycling of nutrients between living organisms and the earth's physical environment.

biological community—the organisms that live together in the same area.

biological magnification—an increase in the concentration of a poison at successively higher trophic levels of a food chain.

biological pest control—the use of a pest organism's natural enemies (such as predators or parasites) to control its population.

biomass—the total weight of the organisms in a particular area.

carnivores—animals that eat other animals.

cellulose—a fibrous substance in plant cells that humans cannot digest.

chemosynthesis—food production by living organisms using energy stored in chemical compounds.

chlorophyll—a green pigment in plants and certain bacteria that absorbs sunlight energy.

consumers—organisms that eat other organisms in the community.

decomposers—organisms that break down wastes and dead matter, returning their components to the environment.

dioxins—chlorine-containing hydrocarbons that are toxic by-products of the manufacture of pesticides and are common pollutants in lakes and other waters.

ecological pyramids—pyramid-shaped diagrams showing the relative numbers, biomass (weight), or energy content of organisms at different trophic levels in an ecosystem; also called Eltonian pyramids.

ecology—the science dealing with the interdependent relationships among organisms and their habitat.

ecosystem—a biological community, in which organisms live and interact with each other and their environment.

essential amino acids—the amino acids that humans cannot produce and must obtain from food.

food chain—a sequence of organisms, each of which is eaten by the next member in the chain.

food web—the interconnected food chains in an ecosystem.

herbivores—animals that eat mainly plants.

heterotrophs—organisms that cannot make their own food and feed on other organisms or their products; they include consumers and decomposers.

integrated farming—a method using the waste products of one agricultural industry as fertilizer or fuel for another, resulting in minimal pollution of the environment.

keystone species—a species essential for the survival of a particular biological community.

lacto-ovo-vegetarian—pertaining to a diet including dairy foods and eggs but no other animal flesh.

niche—the specific role of an organism in a community; its place in the ecosystem or way of living.

nitrogen fixers—bacteria that convert nitrogen gas from the atmosphere to nitrogen compounds that can be used by plants.

omnivores—animals that eat both plants and animals.

ovo-vegetarian—pertaining to a diet including eggs but no dairy foods or animal flesh.

PCBs—polychlorinated biphenyls: toxic industrial by-products that are common water pollutants.

pesco-vegetarian—pertaining to a diet including dairy foods, eggs, and fish, but no other animal flesh.

pesticides—poisonous chemicals used to kill or control insects or other pest organisms.

photosynthesis—a process in which living organisms use sunlight energy to make carbohydrates from carbon dioxide and water, producing oxygen as a by-product.

phytoplankton—single-celled plant-like organisms that live in the surface waters of the oceans.

predators—animals that hunt and kill other animals for food; they are secondary or higher-level consumers.

prey—animals that are killed by other animals for food; they include primary consumers and some secondary consumers.

primary consumer—an organism that feeds on a primary producer; also called a first-level consumer; usually a herbivore.

primary producer—the first link in a food chain, which directly or indirectly provides food for the whole chain.

producers—organisms that make their own food and provide food for other organisms in the ecosystem.

pyramid of biomass—pyramid-shaped diagram showing the relative biomass (weight) of organisms at different trophic levels in an ecosystem.

pyramid of energy—pyramid-shaped diagram showing the relative energy content of organisms at different trophic levels in an ecosystem.

pyramid of numbers—pyramid-shaped diagram showing the relative numbers of organisms at different trophic levels in an ecosystem.

quaternary consumer—an organism that feeds on a tertiary consumer; also called a fourth-level consumer.

rad—a unit of radiation, calculated according to the amount of energy absorbed by living tissue.

respiration—a process in living cells in which carbohydrates and other organic carbon compounds are reacted with oxygen, releasing energy and producing carbon dioxide as a waste product.

scavengers—animals that feed on dead animals or wastes of other organisms.

secondary consumer—an organism that feeds on a primary consumer; also called a second-level consumer; usually a carnivore or an omnivore.

semi-vegetarian—pertaining to a diet including dairy foods, eggs, chicken, and fish, but no other animal flesh.

tertiary consumer—an organism that feeds on a secondary consumer; also called a third-level consumer.

toxin—a poison.

trophic levels—feeding level; the position of a link in a food chain relative to the other links.

umbrella species—a species whose preservation will also protect the other members of its biological community.

vegan—pertaining to a diet consisting only of plant foods, with no animal foods of any kind.

vegetarian—a person who eats a diet of foods derived from plants, and who does not eat meat.

FOR FURTHER INFORMATION

BOOKS

Anderson, Margaret J., Food Chains: The Unending Cycle. Hillside, NJ: Enslow Publishers, 1991.

Hemsley, William, Feeding to Digestion: Projects with Biology. New York: Franklin Watts, 1992.

Kalman, Bobbie, What Are Food Chains & Webs? New York: Crabtree Publishing Company, 1997.

Manning, Mick and Brita Granstrom, Yum-Yum! New York: Franklin Watts, 1997.

Pringle, Laurence, Chains, Webs, and Pyramids: The Flow of Energy in Nature. New York: Thomas Y. Crowell, 1975.

INTERNET RESOURCES

http://ceres.ca.gov/coastalcomm/web/wetrev/wetfig9.html ("Diagram of a Wetland Food Chain")

http://library.advanced.org/11353/food.htm ("The Food Chain": definitions, role of humans; audio discussion)

http://science.coe.uwf.edu/SH/Curr/foodchain/foodchain.htm and
http://science.coe.uwf.edu/SH/Curr/foodweb/foodweb.htm ("Food
Chains" and "Food Webs": definitions, color illustrations, glossary, interactive game)

http://detnews.com/1997/nation/9708/10/0810036.htm ("El Nino's early
arrival disrupts food chain," by William Claiborne: article from The Detroit
News, August 10, 1997)

http://forensicfiles.bc.sympatico.ca/0069.html ("Forensic Files: Poaching
bears affect more than just the population of bears...": ecosystem background and diagrams of North American Black Bear Food Web and North
American Domestic Dog Food Web)

http://udel.edu/~16646 ("Welcome to the Food Pyramid": The USDA Food
Pyramid with "MATCH UP" game and information on fast foods)

http://waisqvarsa.er.usgs.gov/public/wid/FS_216-95/FS_216-95.html
("Mercury Contamination of Aquatic Ecosystems": U.S. Geological Survey
report on mercury in the food chain, with illustrations)

http://www.arco.com/AWE/clep/foodchn.htm ("Food Chains: A Sample
Activity": a Community Education Program Activity to develop an understanding of the basic biotic elements of an ecosystem and their interdependency)

http://www.arts.ouc.bc.ca/geog/G111/4e.html ("Food Chain as a System"),
http://www.arts.ouc.bc.ca/geog/G111/8k.html ("Grazing Food Chain"), and
http://www.arts.ouc.bc.ca/geog/G210/210-2-2-5.html ("Energy Flow in
Ecosystems and Productivity": illustrated materials from courses at the
Department of Geography, Okanagan University College)

http://www.bev.net/education/SeaWorld/Pinnipeds/oneforyou.html
("One for You, Two for Me": activity based on food chains of seals, sea
lions, and walruses)

http://www.cotf.edu/ETE/scen/MSESE/earthsysflr/bio_activity.html
("Mesozoic Food Chain": activity based on dinosaur food chains) and

http://www.cotf.edu/ETE/scen/MSESE/earthsysflr/bio_activity.html
("Middle Latitude Food Chain": interactive food chain activity)

http://www.earthsky.com/1996/mi/esmi960406.html ("More information
on Ocean Food Chain": author's notes from Earth & Sky program)

http://www.hooverdam.com/educate/edpack2.html ("Hoover Dam Teacher/Student Learning Packet: Wildlife": background on the desert ecosystem)

http://www.iit.edu/~smile/bi9002.html ("The Effects of Pesticides on the Food Chain": instructions for student activities, grade 4)

http://www.intercom.net/local/weeg/antarct7.html ("Who Eats Who in the Antarctic?": instructional module, junior high)

http://www.kdu.com/food.html ("A Cave's Food Chain": student activities based on Kentucky Caverns ecosystem)

http://www.miamisci.org/avocado/projects/foodchain/ ("The Food Chain (Let the Sun Shine In)": a Miami elementary school class's description of their food chain projects)

http://www.mucc.org/nature.html ("Natural Discovery": Michigan University monthly wildlife features with background, illustrations, quizzes, puzzles, and games)

http://www.noaa.gov/public-affairs/pr96/mar96/noaa96-11.html ("Zebra Mussels Changing Great Lakes Ecosystem," by Dane Konop and Michael Quigley)

http://www.igc.apc.org/nwf/wlifweek/web1.html ("NATURE'S WEB™Activity One: The Web of Life": National Wildlife Foundation activity illustrating interconnections among elements of the local natural community; grades K-6)

http://www.pbm.com/~lindahl/fchain.html ("Food Chain": an open-ended simulation game of evolving species. Players design animal species that compete against each other in the jungle; play via e-mail)

http://www.public.iastate.edu/~jlmc/escan/Woods/Animals.html ("ESCAN: Animals of the Woodland": illustrated background on the ecosystem of an Iowa woodland)

http://www.rain.org/~losmar/whoeats.htm ("Who Eats Who In The Ocean": making a food chain wall hanging; Science Fair ideas); similar activity at http://www.sd5.k12.mt.us/glaciereft/foodch35.htm "Create a Food Chain, 3-5")

http://www.seattletimes.com/extra/browse.html97/altfert_071997.html
("'Toxic waste in food chain' decried" by Tom Brown, article from Seattle
Times, July 19, 1997)

http://www.veg.org/veg/Orgs/Viva/News/madcow2.html ("Update to
'How Now Mad Cow?'":   discussion of mad cow disease from Viva, April
1996)

http://www.vrg.org/   ("The Vegetarian Resource Group (VRG)":   recipes,
nutrition information, and Vegetarian Game)

http://www.westergaard.com:8080/Notes/meat.html ("Up And Down The
Food Chain":   step-by-step economics of the cattle growing/meat-packing
industry, from a New York Times article, October 17, 1995)

http://www1.npm.ac.uk/set97/foodchai.htm ("Phytoplankton fuel marine
food chains":   colorful illustration of marine food chains)

INDEX